Martin Taylor:

LATIN JAZZ
RHYTHM GUITAR

Rhythm Guitar Comping on Essential Latin Jazz Standards for Guitar

MARTIN TAYLOR

With Tim Pettingale

FUNDAMENTAL CHANGES

Martin Taylor: Latin Jazz Rhythm Guitar

Rhythm Guitar Comping on Essential Latin Jazz Standards for Guitar

ISBN: 978-1-78933-390-9

Published by **www.fundamental-changes.com**

www.fundamental-changes.com

Over 13,000 fans on Facebook: **FundamentalChangesInGuitar**

Instagram: **FundamentalChanges**

For over 350 Free Guitar Lessons with Videos Check Out

www.fundamental-changes.com

Cover Image Copyright: Author photo, used by permission

Contents

About the Authors

Dr Martin Taylor MBE is a virtuoso guitarist, composer, educator and musical innovator.

Acoustic Guitar magazine has called him, "THE acoustic guitarist of his generation." Chet Atkins said that Martin is, "One of the greatest and most impressive guitarists in the world," and Pat Metheny commented that, "Martin Taylor is one of the most awesome solo guitar players in the history of the instrument."

Widely considered to be the world's foremost exponent of solo jazz and fingerstyle guitar playing, Martin possesses an inimitable style that has earned him global acclaim from fellow musicians, fans and critics alike. He dazzles audiences with a signature style which artfully combines his virtuosity, emotion and humour with a strong, engaging stage presence.

Martin has enjoyed a remarkable musical career spanning five decades, with more than 100 recordings to his credit. Completely self-taught, beginning at the early age of 4, he has pioneered a unique way of approaching solo jazz guitar that he now breaks down into seven distinct stages in order to teach others.

Martin has penned many tuition books for the guitar including:

Beyond Chord Melody

Walking Bass for Jazz Guitar

Martin Taylor Single Note Soloing for Jazz Guitar

Martin Taylor's Christmas Songs for Jazz Guitar

Martin Taylor's Complete Jazz Guitar Method Compilation

Martin Taylor's Jazz Guitar Licks Phrase Book

Martin Taylor's Advanced Jazz Guitar Licks Phrase Book

Tim Pettingale is an award-winning author, editor and guitarist who has been involved in international publishing for almost 25 years. He is the author of five bestselling jazz guitar tuition books, and has collaborated on publishing projects with some of the world's most respected players including, Mike Stern, Oz Noy, Ulf Wakenius, Robben Ford, Josh Smith, John Patitucci, Allen Hinds, Steve Morse and many more. He is grateful to have had not one but two great jazz guitar mentors over the years: Adrian Ingram and Dr Martin Taylor MBE.

Introduction from Martin

During my early days as a working musician, I often played at the dance functions that took place in hotel ballrooms across central London. Regularly on the setlist were tunes like *The Girl from Ipanema* and *Meditation* and I noticed that these tunes would always receive a warm response from the audience. Something about the sunny yet relaxed feel of the bossa nova really connected with people. Although I didn't do these kinds of gigs for long, as a jazz musician I grew to love the bossa – not just for its infectious rhythm, but because all the bossa standards have beautiful melodies and chord changes, which makes them fun to improvise over.

Years later, I worked with the guitarist Charlie Byrd in the group The Great Guitars. Charlie was a kind of musicologist who knew all about the music of South America, and had especially fallen in love with the music of Brazil. He, along with other important musicians of his era, was instrumental in bringing this sound to North America. His famous recordings with Stan Getz helped to popularize the form with a wider audience. To this day, if I want to create a summery, laid-back mood in our home when friends come over for dinner, I'll put on some Stan Getz and Charlie Byrd, or maybe Laurindo Almeida, for the mood their music instantly conjures up.

It's important to understand that the bossa nova can be played in dozens of subtly different ways. In fact, there are as many variations of it as there are dialects across South America, and this essentially comes down to the culture/temperament of the people in its different regions. Even within the same nation, the bossa nova of say, Sao Paolo in Brazil, is different from that of Rio de Janeiro.

In jazz, we play a homogenised bossa. It's not the most authentic representation of this music, but it's an adapted way of playing it that just "fits" when jazz musicians come together. When you're on a gig and someone calls a bossa, the way of playing it you'll learn here will always work.

So, this book is *not* the definitive guide to bossa nova, and I don't want you to think this is the "correct" or only way of playing it. Instead, think of it as a way of accessing this music and learning it in a jazz setting. For any purists who are interested in getting into Latin music in more detail, I encourage you to listen to and study the music of guitar players who grew up and developed their craft in South America. For example, check out the incredible playing of Yamandú Costa, the Brazilian 7-string virtuoso. He's one of my favourite players of this type of music!

As you work through the examples here, remember that the main thing about the bossa nova is the *feel*. Learn the chord voicings and the rhythms, but above all, strive to capture the summery, laid-back vibe. Once you have that in place, you can explore all the different ways there are to embellish the rhythm and elevate it into something more sophisticated.

In Chapter One, I'll show you the basic bossa nova rhythm, then we'll quickly move on to explore how to elaborate on it to make things more interesting. Once you've got the hang of playing simple embellishments, in the chapters that follow we'll apply those principles to some well-known bossa nova standards, then we'll end the book with a surprise arrangement! The tunes in this book were chosen because they are the pieces most requested by my students, who often ask me how they should approach them. I hope you learn a lot from them.

Enjoy this little Latin Jazz journey!

Martin.

Get the Audio

The audio files for this book are available to download for free from **www.fundamental-changes.com.** The link is in the top right-hand corner. Click on the "Guitar" link then simply select this book title from the drop-down menu and follow the instructions to get the audio.

We recommend that you download the files directly to your computer, not to your tablet, and extract them there before adding them to your media library. You can then put them onto your tablet, iPod or burn them to CD. On the download page there are instructions, and we also provide technical support via the contact form.

For over 350 free guitar lessons with videos check out:

www.fundamental-changes.com

Join our free Facebook Community of Cool Musicians

www.facebook.com/groups/fundamentalguitar

Tag us for a share on Instagram: **FundamentalChanges**

Chapter One – The Basic Jazz Bossa Nova Rhythm

When we talk about *Latin Jazz*, we really mean a jazz tune played with either a samba or bossa nova rhythm (a bossa is essentially a slow samba). Jam sessions will nearly always include tunes like *Blue Bossa* (bossa) and *St Thomas* (samba) along with many others. Overwhelmingly, the bossa nova is the more popular of the two, and there are many more tunes written for it, so it's essential to have a good grasp of this rhythm and to understand what can be done to elevate it into something a bit more special.

As mentioned in the introduction, there are many variations of the bossa rhythm. All bossa nova's have a basic *feel* and *groove* that is similar, but depending on where a musician grew up, it might be played with different *accents* – small inflections that are peculiar to a specific region.

To account for this, jazz musicians tend to play a simplified bossa that captures the essence of the rhythm and is acceptable across the spectrum of jazz music. It may have moved away somewhat from a purist's view of authentic bossa nova, but its pulse and feel are immediately recognisable.

In this chapter you'll learn the basic bossa nova rhythm and get familiar with the chord forms that are used when playing it.

To illustrate, we'll use the chord sequence from the first eight bars of the popular tune *The Girl from Ipanema* by Antônio Carlos Jobim. In turn, we'll look at:

1. The basic chord shapes used in this type of music (which allow for easy movement of the bass note to create the bossa rhythm)

2. How to play the basic bossa rhythm

3. How to embellish the basic rhythm with bass note movements

4. How to add more movement to the chords with upper string embellishments

Let's get started!

Chord shapes

The bossa rhythm has two main characteristics:

1. A steady bassline pattern that alternates between bass notes on the bottom two strings.

2. Chord accents that are mostly played in counterpoint to the bass notes.

In order to play the alternating bassline (and to add embellishments later) we need to allow a spare finger, so all the chord shapes tend to be simple, four-note forms, with a few exceptions.

While we're learning the rhythm we'll play the "Ipanema" changes in the key of C Major. Below are the five chord shapes you'll need.

All the chords used in this book are moveable shapes. The root notes are indicated below, so you can easily transpose them to other keys.

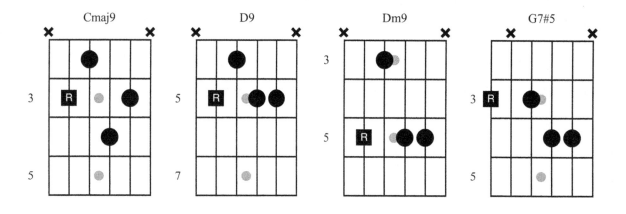

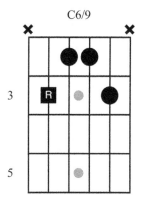

Notice that the chords are all arranged on the inner four strings. This leaves the low and high E strings free for adding embellishments.

First, play through the chords and listen to how they sound in Example 1a.

Example 1a

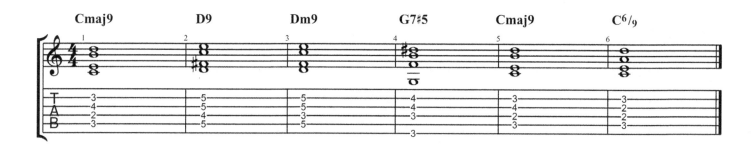

Using just the Cmaj9 chord to begin with, we'll set up and practice the basic bossa rhythm. This rhythm will form the foundation of everything you play in this book, so we'll spend a bit of time on it. First, have a listen to the audio for Example 1b several times and fix the sound of the rhythm in your head.

In a moment, I'll break down exactly how the bossa nova rhythm is put together, beat by beat, but first an important word about the picking hand.

Your thumb is going to take care of the bass notes on the fifth and sixth strings, while your first, second and third fingers take care of plucking the rest of the chord on strings 4, 3 and 2.

Think of the movement of your thumb and fingers as a *pinching motion*, with the thumb plucking downwards and the fingers plucking upwards. You'll use this motion all the time from now on, sometimes plucking down/up simultaneously on the beat, and sometimes plucking upwards on the off-beat.

Now, have a look through the example you're about to play and familiarise yourself with the movement the thumb will make, moving between the bottom two strings.

Example 1b

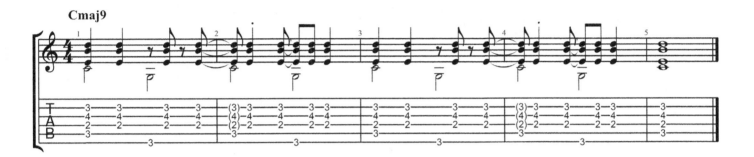

This rhythm is a two-bar pattern. Let's break it down and see what's happening. There are a few important things to notice.

Bar One

First of all, notice that the bass notes always fall on beats 1 and 3 of the bar. They are like the "metronome of bossa". The bass notes form a steady pulse, while the chord plucks create the syncopation.

- On beat 1, play the fifth string bass note and upward pluck the chord at the same time in a pinching motion

- On beat 2, just play an upward chord pluck, don't play the bass note

- On beat 3, play just the bass note, which has now hopped over onto the sixth string

Now for the syncopated accents:

- An upward chord pluck is played on beat 3&

- An upward chord pluck is played on beat 4&

Notice that this last chord pluck is allowed to ring, so that it carries over into the beginning of bar two.

Play just bar one and make sure you're getting all the accents in the right places.

Bar Two

We're still hitting the bass notes on beats 1 and 3 of bar two, but there's no upward chord pluck on beat 1 because it was played at the very end of bar one.

Now the pattern differs from bar one with two offbeat chord plucks:

- On beat 1& play an upward chord pluck

- On beat 2& play an upward chord pluck

- On beat 3, play the sixth string bass note

- On beat 3& play an upward chord pluck

- On beat 4 play an upward chord pluck

Listen to the audio one more time to hear how this sounds.

That's a lot of information to take in, but I've spelled it out for you here so that you can refer back to it if you need to. Bossa is best heard and felt, so let the audio be your guide.

Play through Example 1b again. First make sure you're consistently hitting the bass notes on beats 1 and 3, then ensure you're playing the chord accents on the correct beats.

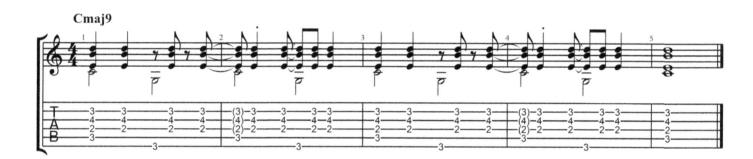

It's this mixture of on and off-beat accents that gives the bossa nova its characteristic lilting groove. Play Example 1b as many times as you need to lock in the rhythm, because next you're going to begin changing chords. If you embed this rhythm in your ears, it'll become second nature, and you'll be able to comp your way through any bossa nova jazz tune and only have to worry about reading the chords.

Now it's time to apply this rhythm to the chord changes of *The Girl from Ipanema*.

We're using the basic rhythm pattern from the previous example, but I've made a tiny modification to it. Occasionally I'll sneak in an extra bass note pluck on beat 2&. This is completely optional, and you can leave it out for now if you like.

Also, in bar six I've added a Db9 chord (I can't help it, I'm a jazz musician!). This is a common chord substitution idea in jazz, where one dominant chord is substituted with another a flat fifth above it. In bar six, the original chord was G7 and Db9 is the dominant chord a b5 interval above it. This happens again in bar eight. As well as being a common substitution, the Db9 is also easier to play after the Dm9 because you can move to it without changing your grip on the neck.

You'll see this idea crop up in the other bossa tunes as we move on.

First concentrate on the bassline movements, practicing them with the thumb, and making sure to keep the metronomic feel going on beats 1 and 3. Next, focus on the chord accents and moving smoothly between chords.

Example 1c

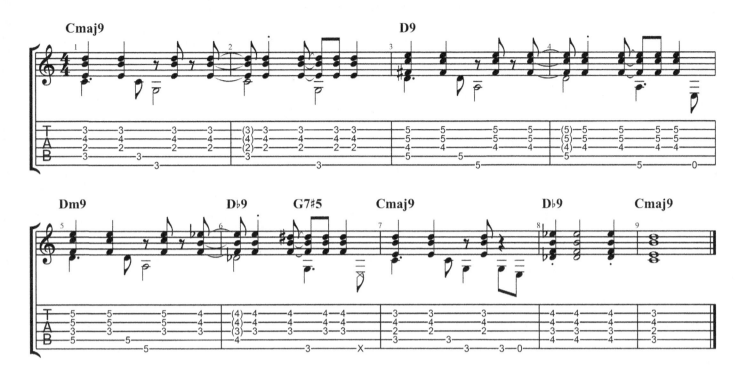

Spend some time looping Example 1c until you have a steady groove locked in. The aim is to maintain a smooth bossa rhythm while changing chords, which can be trickier than it sounds. Feel free to learn it slower than the tempo on the audio to lock in the movements, then bring it up to speed.

Chord accent variations

You now have the basic bossa rhythm in place. At this point, I advise you to get out the Real Book and play any tune you like as a relaxed bossa. It might be *Autumn Leaves, My Funny Valentine* or whatever you choose – most tunes can adapt to the bossa treatment. Just keep practicing the basic rhythm until you can do it in your sleep.

When you've got that down, it's time to decorate the rhythm, and for the rest of this chapter I want to show you some different variations you can use to make things more interesting. Remember that the bass notes on 1 and 3 are the bossa metronome. I may occasionally move a bass note accent, but the majority of them will stay on beats 1 and 3.

In a moment you'll play Example 1d – a complete eight-bar sequence – but first I want to break it into three smaller chunks to talk about what's happening at different points.

In bars 1-2, I've made some subtle changes to freshen things up. I've used a C6/9 chord rather than Cmaj9 because it has a brighter sound, which immediately lifts the mood.

At the end of bar one, I don't allow the chord upstroke to ring into bar two. Instead, it's cut off, and at the beginning of bar two there is a rest. Before we had a chord sounding on beat 1 of bar two, but now there is silence until we play the upstroke on beat 1&. This simple change is quite effective and noticeably adds to the syncopation of the groove.

11

The rest of bar two is different too. It highlights one of the few occasions where the bass note *doesn't* fall on beat 3. Instead, the bass note anticipates the beat and the upstroke lands on beat 3. I've also made the last two upstrokes in bar two 1/4 notes rather than 1/8th notes to change the feel a little more.

Listen to the audio of Example 1d and take a moment to process how these small variations affect the overall feel and syncopation of the rhythm.

More rhythmic variations are introduced in bars 3-4 for the D9 chord. This time, in bar three I chose to play 1/8th note chord accents to create a quicker "1 and 2 and" rhythm. In the second half of bar three, I added in an extra bass note movement to keep things moving.

Notice the X symbol here. Bossa nova rhythm guitarists are really copying what a Latin percussionist would play, and occasionally I play a sound which is more a percussive hit on the strings than an actual note. (I snuck one of these in at the end of the previous example). Just keep fretting whatever chord you're playing and tap your thumb very lightly against the strings.

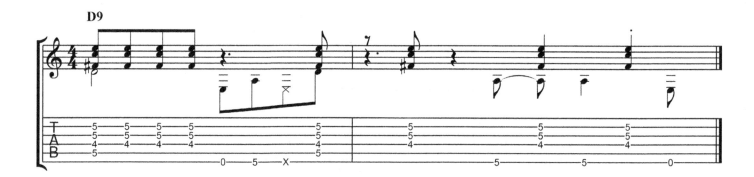

The final four bars of Example 1d are closer to the basic rhythm, but I alternate between playing a chord on beat 1 of the bar and a leaving a rest.

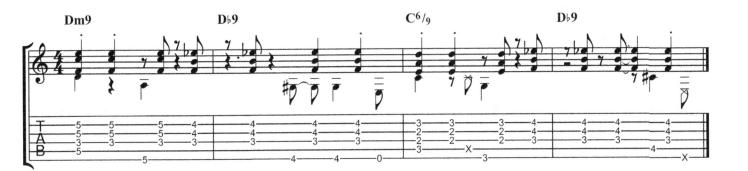

Now we've broken down what's going on, we'll combine the previous three ideas and play them together in Example 1d. This gives us an interesting rhythm accompaniment that keeps the bossa feel but adds subtle embellishments to the chord accents.

Example 1d

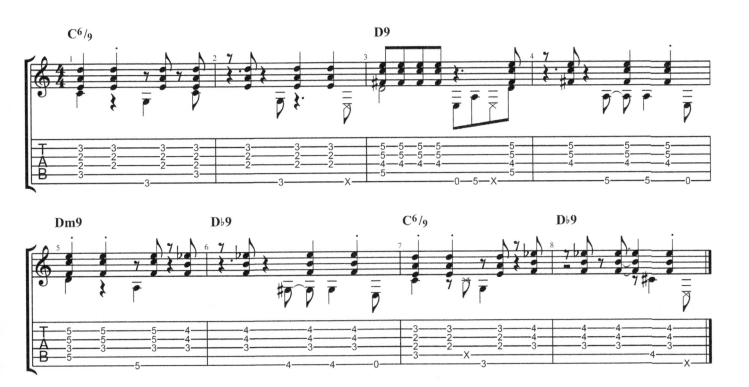

Taking the ideas we've learned so far, the next example is an alternative take on the eight-bar sequence. There is a little bassline variation here in bar two.

Example 1e

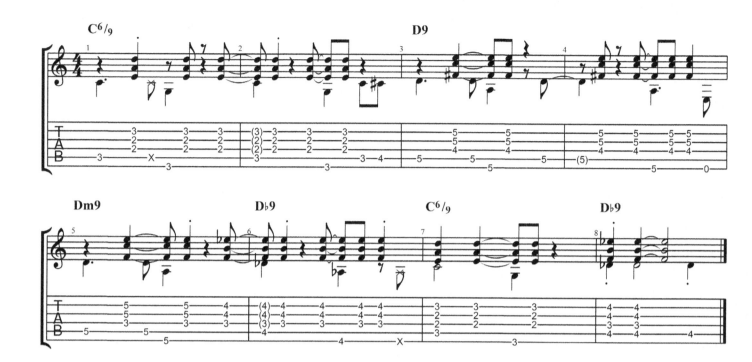

Bar two of the next example shows a simple way of adding energy to the chord changes. At the end of bar two I anticipate the D9 chord in bar three by approaching it from a half step below (Db9). At the end of bars three and five, I let the chords ring and sustain into the next bar.

Example 1f

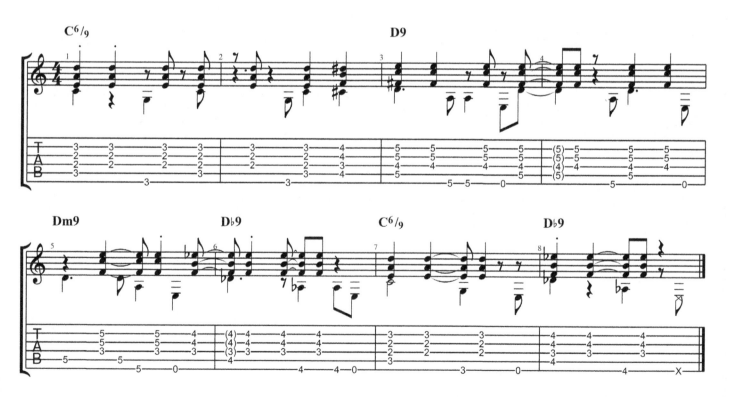

Here's a different, more attention-grabbing way of changing the bossa rhythm that I like to play from time to time. In bar one, I move away from the bossa pulse to play chords that cut against the groove. On beat 1, the C6/9 chord is played as a dotted 1/4 note, which means it sounds for one and a half beats.

This unexpected sustained chord is followed by two more dotted 1/4 notes, both of which anticipate the beat. The first sounds just before beat 3, and the second anticipates beat 1 of bar two.

The same idea occurs in bar four, but the chord repeats are straight 1/4 notes, which varies the rhythm again. In bars 5-8 we drop back into the conventional bossa rhythm.

Example 1g

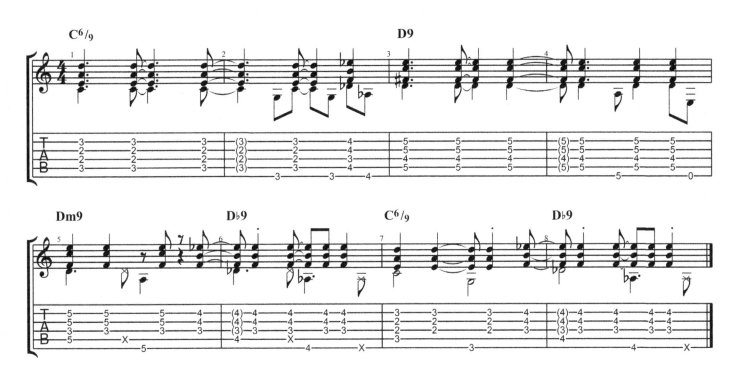

Something you'll often hear in band arrangements of bossa tunes is accents played in unison by the whole group. It's a good way to change up the bossa feel to create rhythmic interest for the audience, but we can apply the same idea to a solo guitar accompaniment for dramatic effect.

In bars 1-5 we play these 1/8th note stabs on each chord change, then begin to move back to a standard bossa rhythm in bar six.

Example 1h

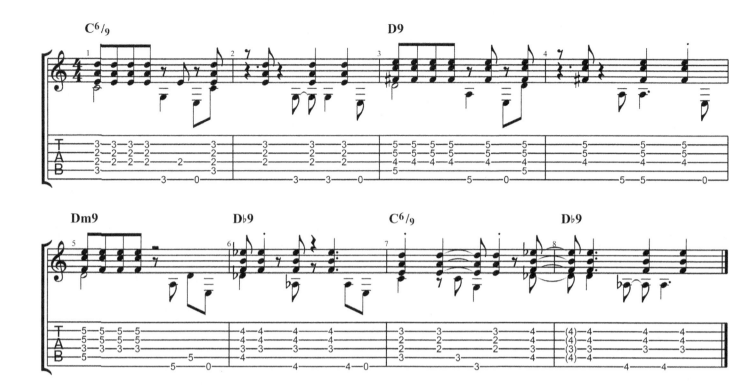

Bassline embellishments

As a rhythm guitarist, an effective way to add interest to your part is by varying the bassline, and the next few examples illustrate different ways in which we can do this. Don't forget we're playing a bossa nova, so we don't want to go crazy, but that doesn't mean our part has to be boring.

To begin with, we can add short runs that target bass notes, as at the end of bar two below. Here, I play one passing note that connects the root of the C6/9 chord to the root of D9.

Another simple thing we can do is to *push* against the groove by playing notes a little early or late. Playing a note early creates momentum, while playing behind the beat creates a more laidback feel.

In bar five, instead of keeping the bass notes just on beats 1 and 3, I play a D note on the fifth string on beat 4&. This serves two purposes: first, it immediately breaks up the metronomic rhythm and the ear is drawn to it. Second, it resolves down a half step to the Db note that falls on beat 1 of bar six.

Example 1i

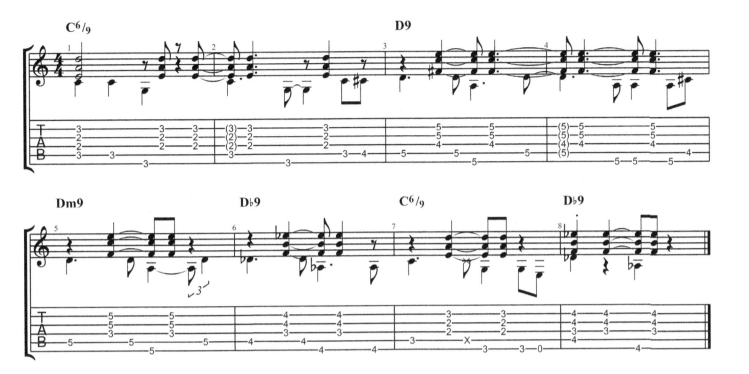

Here's another example of pushing against the groove to give more energy to the accompaniment. In bar one you'll notice that the first bass note on the sixth string is played on beat 2& rather than 3. Anticipating the bass note like this has a big effect on the feel.

In bar two, I repeat the bass notes to create a brief walking bassline. Then, in bars 5-8, each time the Db bass note is played on the fifth string, it's placed before the beat.

Example 1j

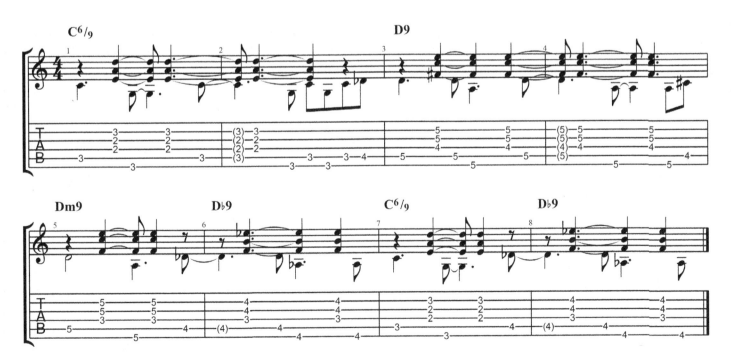

Here's a more elaborate variation of the previous example. In bar two I've added more notes to the fifth string walking bassline to create a run up to the root note of the D9 chord in bar three.

For bars 5-8, I introduce a new idea to break up the rhythm, which is to play a triplet pattern alternating between the fifth and sixth string bass notes. Listen to the audio to get the timing of this. Every time it's played, it resolves to the root note of the chord that falls on beat 1 of the next bar. If you play the triplet too slowly you won't land nicely on the beat! Use quick thumb downstrokes to play it.

Example 1k

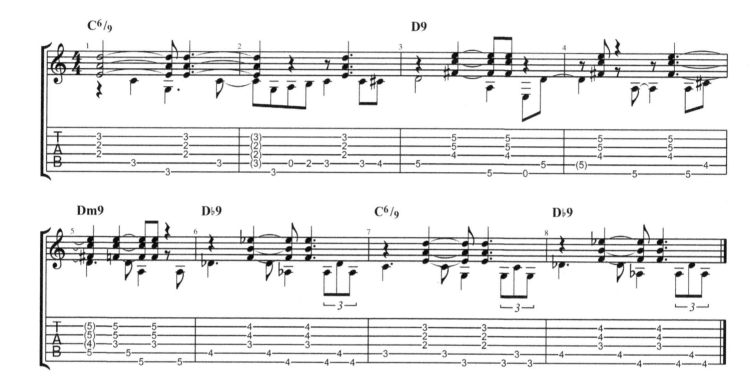

The next example has lots of *pushed* accents that give the bossa rhythm some swing. This example is all about showcasing the bassline and keeping the chord upstrokes simple. In bars 5-8 you'll hear a descending bass note idea on the sixth string and a more colourful sounding Db7#9 chord in bar six.

Example 11

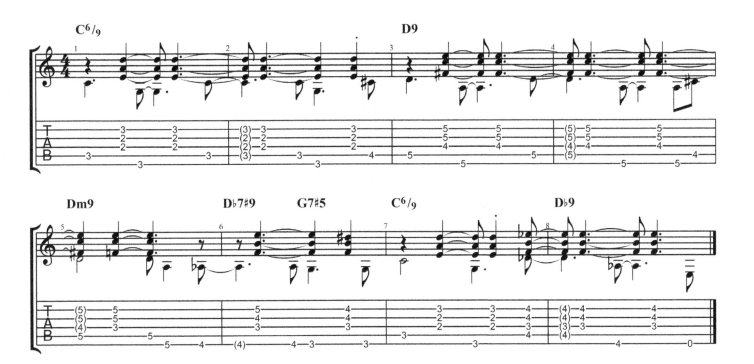

Melodic embellishments

Without forgetting that our role as rhythm guitarist is to accompany and support a vocalist or soloist, there are embellishments we can add to the bossa rhythm that use inner moving lines and high string melodies. We don't want to overuse these ideas while someone is singing the tune, but they are incredibly useful when a soloist is playing, or when we're playing in a duo and we need to take a "solo". In the latter scenario, stopping the rhythm to play single note melodies doesn't work well, so it's good to develop the skill of being able to keep the rhythm going and decorate it with melodic lines.

To begin with, here's a common Latin Jazz embellishment. It's all about moving lines within the chords using easy movements.

In bars 1-2, hold down the Cmaj9 shape throughout. Normally you'd probably play Cmaj9 with your first finger arched to hold down the 2nd fret on the fourth string, but to play this idea it's better to flatten it, so it's barring the fourth and third strings. This allows you to lift your fourth finger from the third string to play the repeating phrase.

A similar idea occurs in bars 3-4 with the D9 chord. This time, you'll move your second finger (which is fretting the root note on the fifth string) across onto the fourth string. Once there, alternate between the 5th and 4th frets to create a phrase. The phrase is the focus of this bar, so notice that the bass notes are *ghost* notes, indicated by the X.

Example 1m

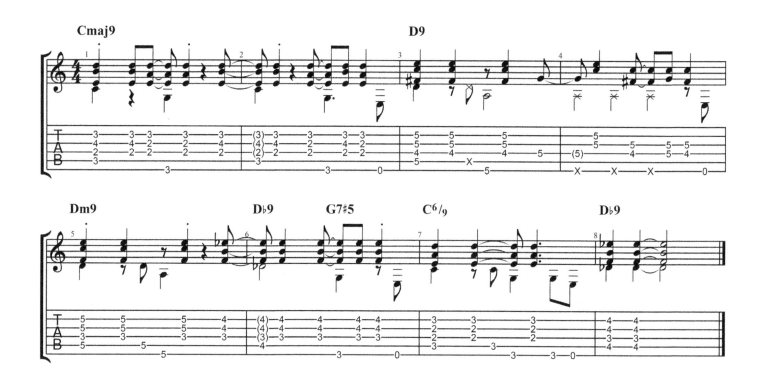

Here's another example of a moving inside line. In bars 1-2, I play what's known as a *shell voicing* of Cmaj7, which is a way of defining the sound of the chord with just three notes (root, 3rd and 7th). This makes it easier to move the notes on the third string to create a chromatic descending phrase.

In bar two, I've included another little device that jazz musicians use to add colour to the chord changes: wherever you see a dominant chord, you can usually pretend that it's a V chord and add the ii chord that would normally precede it – in this case, Am7 to D9. (I could have also added an Abm7 before the Db9 in bar six, if I'd wanted to sound like Charlie Parker playing a bossa!)

In bars 7-8, I play a short embellishment on the higher strings. This is a movement you may have heard me play before, as it's one of my favourite sounds. In bar seven, hold down the full Cmaj7 shape. Then, as we transition into bar eight, turn your first finger into a barre at the 3rd fret and stretch out the third and fourth fingers to fret the notes at the 6th and 7th frets.

If you find the stretch difficult, make sure you're not barring at the 3rd with your first finger completely flat on the fretboard. Barring with the side of your finger will allow you to reach further.

Example 1n

We can introduce sustaining notes on the top strings to bring a different dimension to our rhythm part. In this example you'll see I'm mostly adding notes on the top string, with a couple on the second. The key is to pluck those first string notes a little harder than the rest, using your third finger so that they really pop out. If you get it right, it will sound like two guitars playing separate parts.

In this example you'll see I've replaced the Db9 chord with the original V chord (G7), but I'm playing more colourful G13 and G7#5 voicings.

Example 1o

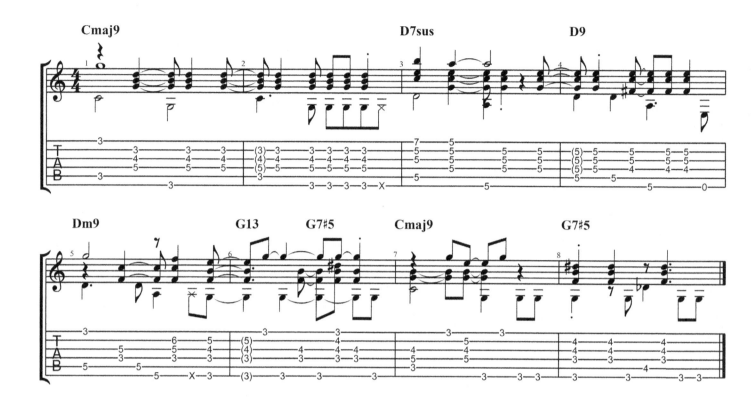

We can develop the melodic idea of the previous example and alter the rhythm to bring a lot more interest and movement. In this example I'm using triplet phrases in bars three and six. Playing triplet rhythms here has the effect of pulling back on the time slightly which makes these chords stand out.

Example 1p

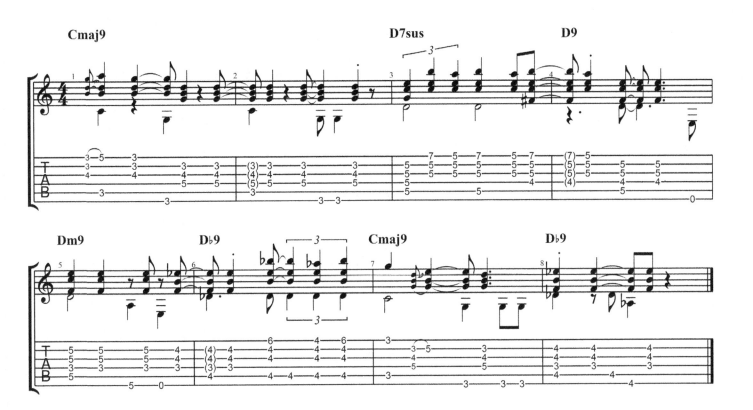

We can keep a melodic motif going, but vary other elements of the rhythm to keep things interesting. Here, I've kept the top string melody, but added some inside movement to the chords on the fourth string.

Example 1q

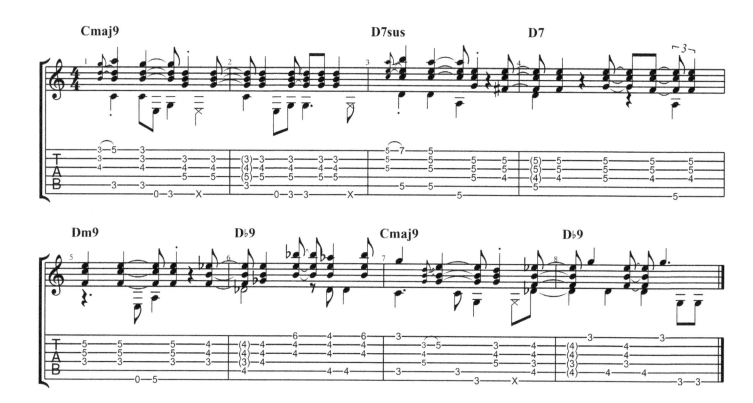

Of course, we can combine all the ideas we've looked at in subtle ways to create unlimited variations in the rhythm part. This example combines a high string melody, some movement on the inside strings, and a busier bass accompaniment.

Example 1r

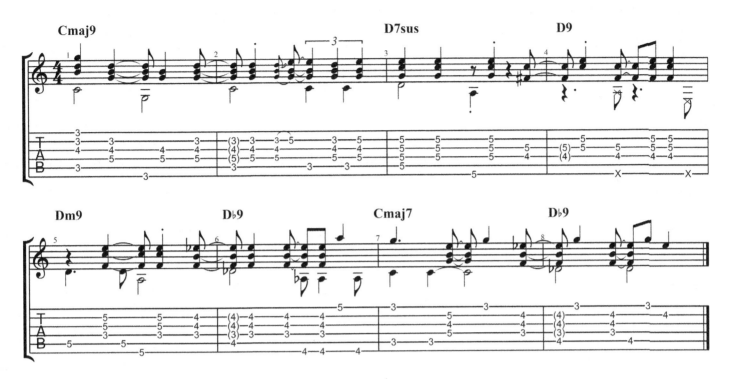

This approach hints at our melodic motif and includes a chromatic descending inner line.

Example 1s

Here's one more variation to end this chapter. I'm playing the chords in a slightly more staccato way and focusing on making the rhythm really groove. I hope you can see that there are endless small changes you can make to your rhythm parts, while still maintaining the groove and feel of the bossa.

Example 1t

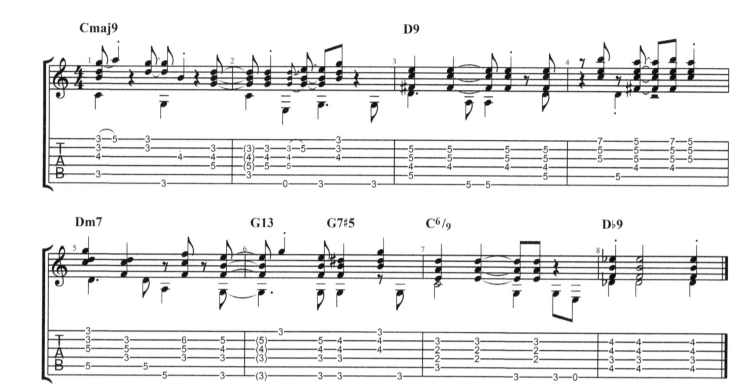

Chapter Two – The Girl from Ipanema

In the chapters that follow, we're going to look at comping ideas for seven tunes that are among the most popular bossa novas ever written. Plus, in the final chapter, you'll learn my bossa arrangement of a very famous Ivor Novella tune from 1914 to show that any great tune can lend itself to this versatile Latin rhythm approach.

Since we've been practicing the bossa nova on the opening changes of *The Girl from Ipanema*, we'll begin with that tune. However, we'll play it in its original key of F Major, so you can use these ideas when jamming with other musicians.

First, we'll look at a few different ways of embellishing the A section chords in this key, because a change of key naturally opens up some different ideas on the fretboard. Then we'll do the same with the B section. At the end of the chapter, there is a full arrangement of comping ideas for you to learn.

When playing these ideas, remember that we're applying *exactly the same principles* you learned in the previous chapter to create the embellishments. We can add:

- Variations to the chord accents

- Bassline movements

- Inner line movements

- Top string melodies

For this reason, I won't give long explanations for each example unless there's something of particular interest.

With the change to the key of F Major, there are a few new chord shapes in use, in addition to the ones you played in Chapter One. For the vast majority of the time, the embellishment ideas will be added around these shapes, and I'll only occasionally break out of them to transition between chords.

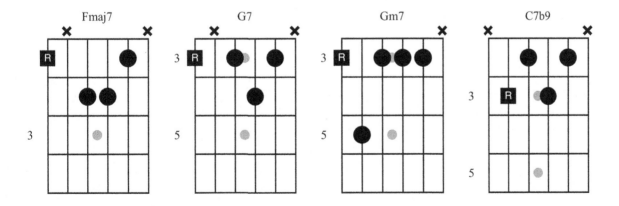

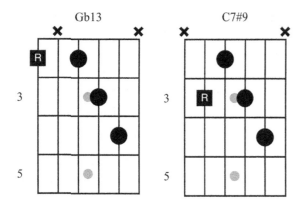

A word on fingerings for the examples in this chapter. Because this tune is in F Major, we're playing some chords that have a sixth string root note. This can mean that we run out of fingers quite quickly, so to free up fingers to play embellishments, I occasionally use my thumb over the neck to fret the sixth string bass notes.

The first example begins with a descending inner line on the fourth string, then moves to a melody on the first string. In bars 1-4, use your thumb for the bass notes. You can play a normal barre chord for the Gm7 to C7b9 movement, then it's back to the thumb for bars 7-8. It might feel a little awkward to use the thumb for Fmaj7 at first, but persevere with it!

Example 2a

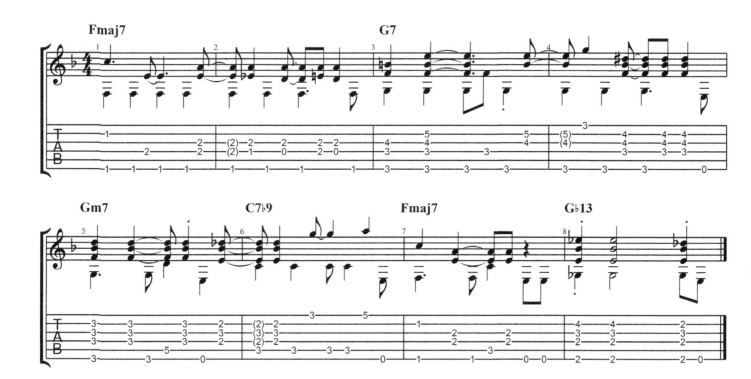

Here's a similar idea with some rhythmic changes.

Example 2b

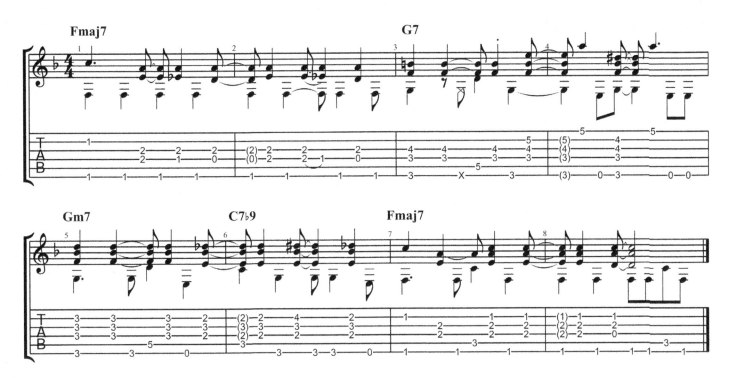

Example 2c combines a slight variation in the chord rhythm and a moving melodic line on the second string.

Example 2c

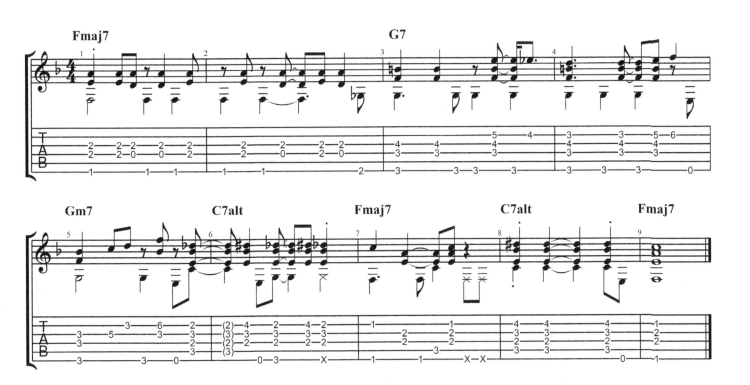

Let's look at the B section of the tune. As it has quite a long form, I've broken it into two halves.

Here's how to play the first eight bars of the B section. I play the Gbmaj7 in bar one, and the Amaj7 in bar five using the thumb for the bass notes. For the chords with a root note on the fifth string (Cb9 and D9), switch back to the method you learned in Chapter One.

Example 2d

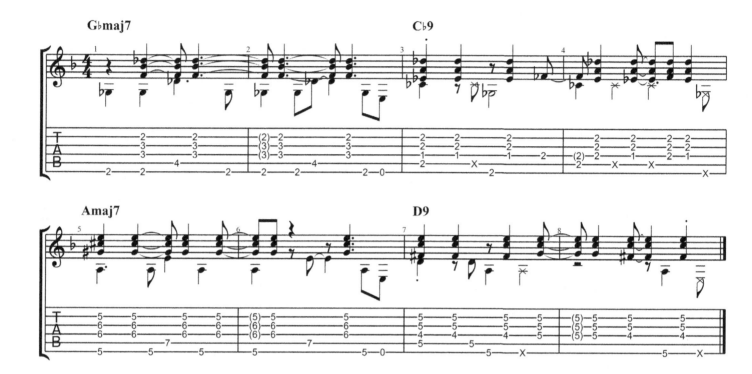

Here are the next eight bars of the B section. Use the thumb to play the bass note of Bbmaj7. When you get to the Am7 in bar five, use a conventional barre shape with your first finger across the 5th fret, and do the same for the Gm7 in bar seven.

Example 2e

Practice the previous examples until you can move smoothly between the shapes. When you're ready, have a go at the full comping arrangement in Example 2f.

Example 2f

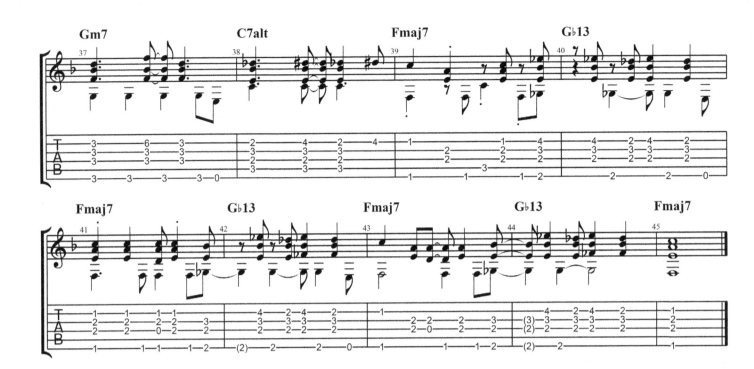

Chapter Three – The Shadow of Your Smile

The Shadow of Your Smile is one of just two songs in this book not written by Antônio Carlos Jobim. The music came from the great Johnny Mandel and lyrics were added by Paul Francis Webster. The song was first heard in 1965 on the soundtrack for the film *The Sandpiper*, starring Elizabeth Taylor and Richard Burton, and it won the Grammy Award for Song of the Year and an Academy Award for Best Original Song. It has since been covered by a huge range of artists from Frank Sinatra to Stevie Wonder.

This tune has an AB format, with each section being 16-bars long. We'll look at each section in turn and also split each one into more manageable eight-bar chunks.

There are three chord shapes we've not used so far in our bossa arrangements. I'm sure you know them very well already, but here they are for completeness.

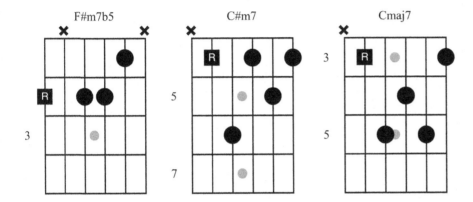

This first example is built around a melodic line on the second string in the first four bars and adds some higher embellishments in the next four. In bar one, we can take advantage of the B note of the open second string to help create the riff.

In bars 3-4, use the thumb to play the 7th fret bass note for Em7, then move to a standard barre chord shape for the Am7 in bar five.

There's quite a lot going on here, so listen to the audio then play through the example slowly to practice your coordination.

Example 3a

Now onto the second half of the A section. Notice that the first four bars use similar chords to bars 1-4 of the previous example, but the composer adds a twist to take the harmony in a different direction for the subsequent four bars.

In bar seven, the original changes stay on the F# chord and change it from F#7 to F#°7 (which creates a minor ii V movement leading to the B7 in bar eight). Instead, I use another of those b5 substitutions which lend themselves so well to Latin Jazz, and play a C9 chord. You'll notice that it's also much easier to play!

Bars 1-4 of this example is where a lot of the embellishment takes place, so carefully work out your fingering movements.

Example 3b

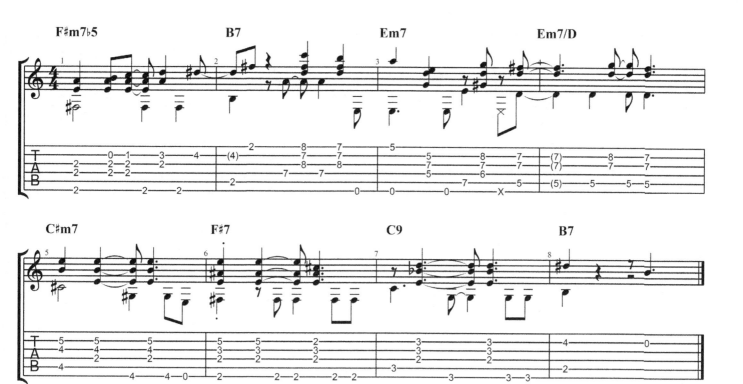

B Section

Now let's look at the B section, again splitting it into eight-bar chunks.

In bar seven I play another common jazz substitution idea which is worth noting.

In jazz, it's very common to shift ideas around the neck in minor 3rds (a distance of three frets). After the D9 chord in bar six, the original chord changes have a B°7, which would set up another minor ii V movement (B°7 – E7alt). Instead, I play the D9 chord then shift it up a minor 3rd to F9. From there, a half step movement downwards gets me to the E7alt chord (in this instance an E7b9).

Experiment with this idea in your playing. It's also very common to shift the ii chord up a minor 3rd in a major ii V I (e.g. Dm7 – G7 – Cmaj7, becomes Dm7 – Fm7 – Cmaj7). Try it!

Example 3c

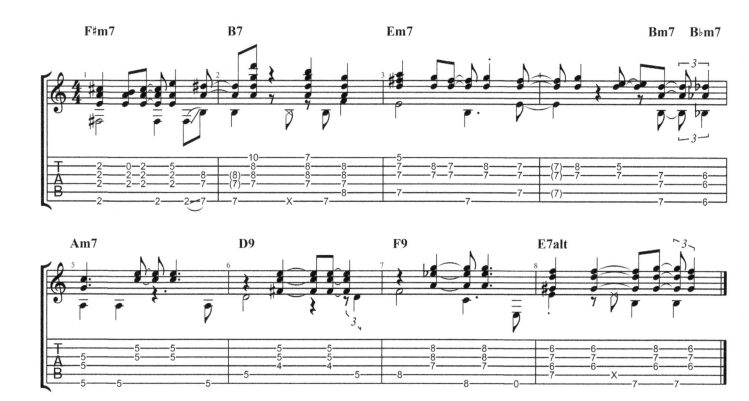

Here's the second half of the B section. Listen to the harmony in bar two. Here, the composer has written a minor 3rd shift (Am7 moving to Cm7). You can hear how this movement dovetails beautifully into the Bm7 chord that follows with a half-step movement.

Example 3d

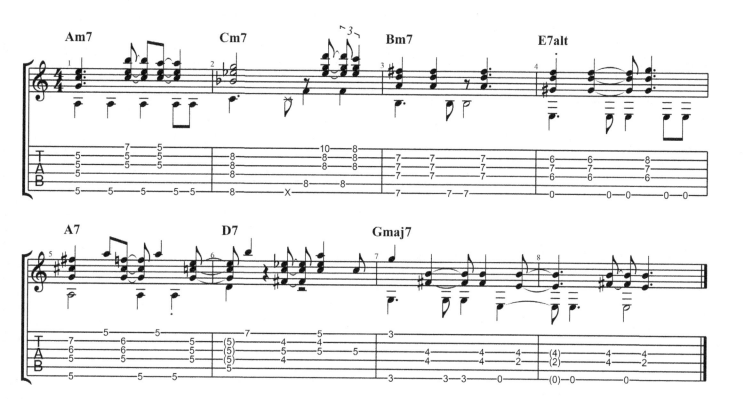

Now you're getting used to the idea of adding embellishments based around specific chord grips, have a go at the full arrangement of *The Shadow of Your Smile*. I've made it a little more challenging to play than the previous chapter's arrangement, so you'll have some work to do in your practice sessions and a goal to work towards.

It's more syncopated than before and I also play with the rhythm at times. Break it down into smaller sections as you work through it.

Example 3e

Chapter Four – Wave

Wave is an ever-popular Jobim tune and was included in the Brazilian edition of *Rolling Stone* in the list of the greatest Brazilian tunes of all time. There are some great recordings of this tune by Jobim himself, Oscar Peterson, Paul Desmond, Sarah Vaughn, Frank Sinatra, McCoy Tyner and many more.

It has been called "Jobim's blues" by students of jazz, because the A section is twelve bars long and has very similar chord changes to Charlie Parker tune *Blues for Alice* (where Parker added lots of additional chord changes and substitution ideas to the standard three chord blues).

The tune follows an AABA format, so we effectively have three lots of bebop blues, with a different, eight-bar B section sandwiched in between. Of course, the bossa nova feel of the rhythm disguises this tune's blues heritage.

We're going to look at comping ideas for this tune in complete sections. The examples that follow show you a few ways to navigate the basic changes in preparation for the full chorus at the end of the chapter.

Most of the chord forms used for this tune are ones you've encountered before. So, when you see a D7 or C9 chord, you know you'll be playing the familiar fifth string root shape, etc. There are just a couple of more exotic voicings I used in this arrangement, which I'll give you chord diagrams for in the examples that follow.

I've made a slight tweak to the harmony of this tune compared to what you'll typically find in the Real Book. In bar two, the original chord is Bb°7 (a b5 substitution that leads into the Am7 in bar three). I like to add an A bass note to this chord, which means we could call it A7b9 (as written above the notation), but bear in mind it's just the original Bb°7 over an A bass note, which adds some nice tension to the harmony.

After the D6/9 voicing at the 5th fret, the chords are arranged on the top strings to allow the open fifth string to keep going throughout bars 1-4. Whenever the open strings notes are right for the tune you're playing, always try to include them. They can be great launch pads to change position quickly to a different area of the neck and are, of course, easy to play.

The best way to grip the Gmaj7 in bar five is to fret the notes on strings 2, 3 and 4, with the first, third and second fingers (in order), and play the bass note with the thumb. This frees up the little finger to play the 5th fret bass note on the fifth string.

Example 4a

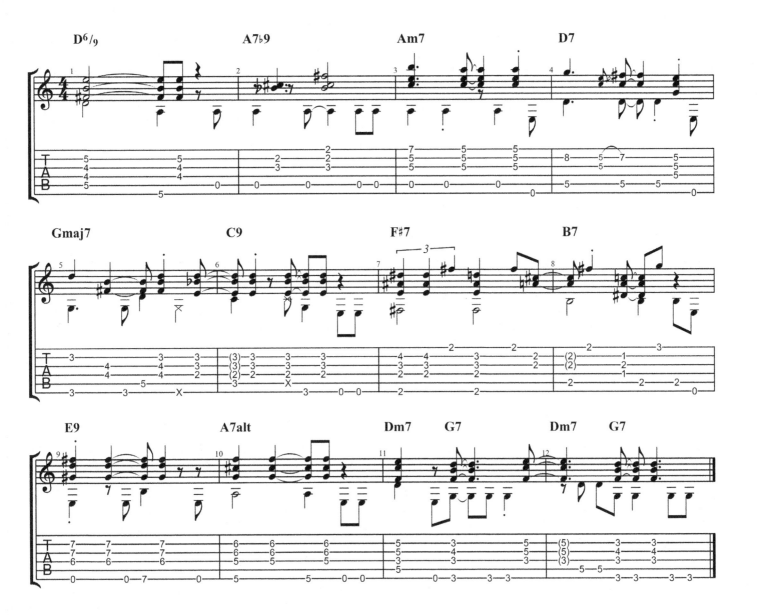

The next time around the A section we can begin to add some variations.

In bars 1-2, I keep the open A string idea going, but move to a barre chord form for the Am7 in bar three. Bars 4-6 are fairly straightforward, but in bar seven you'll need to alter your grip for the F#7 chord at the same time as varying the rhythm.

Start by barring a normal F#7 chord at the 2nd fret. Your fourth finger will play the melody note on the second string.

Now alter your grip to play the second chord (an F#7#5). You first finger will still be barred at the 2nd fret, but your second and third fingers will play the notes on strings 2 and 3. For the last chord in bar seven, release the low E string and play it open, but keep barring the rest of the strings at the 2nd fret. In bar eight, return to a normal grip for the B7 chord.

Example 4b

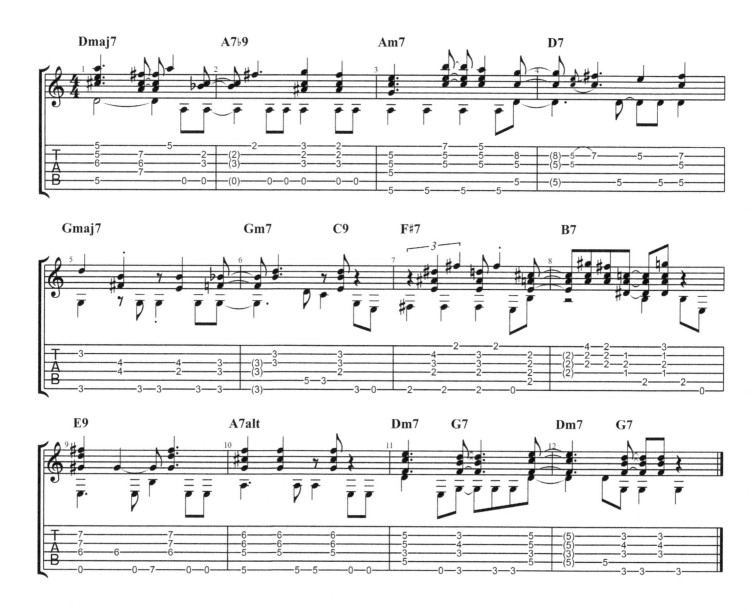

We also need a version of the A section that will lead into the middle eight.

This example begins in a similar way to Example 4a, but in bar three I play an Am7 barre chord to set up an inside descending chromatic line. When playing bossa nova, it's tempting to think we need to constantly be playing that bass pulse or we'll lose the groove, but in fact if we keep the groove going *most* of the time, we can play phrases like this with no bass accompaniment and the listener's ears will simply fill in the blanks.

In bar seven you'll hear a triplet rhythm to create more interest in the groove. This happens again in bar twelve, and here the extra Abm7 chord leads chromatically to the Gm7 chord that begins the B section.

Example 4c

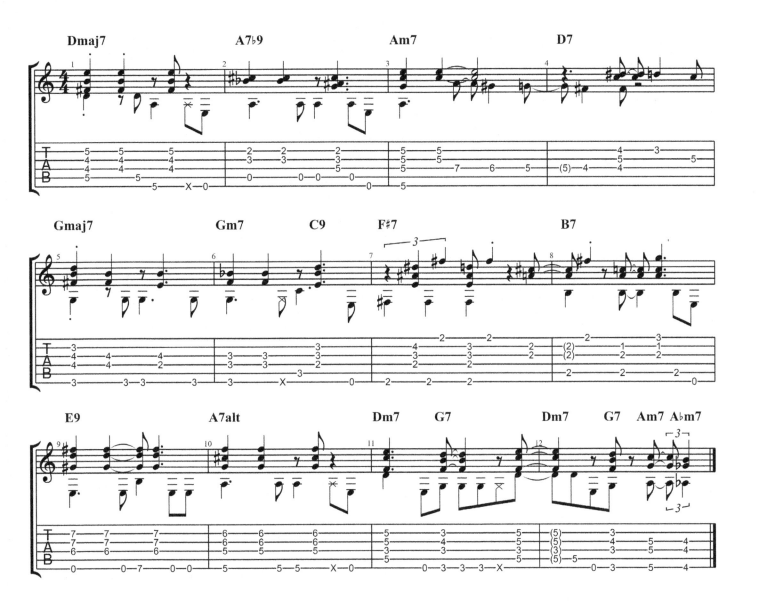

Next, we move on to the B section or middle eight. You've played similar chords to these before, so you'll be using moveable chord shapes you already know.

In bar one, barre with the first finger at the 3rd fret to play Gm7 and release your third finger to play the bass note. Bar three shows how we can create a riff by moving part of a chord on the middle strings to make the Fmaj7 bars more interesting.

Example 4d

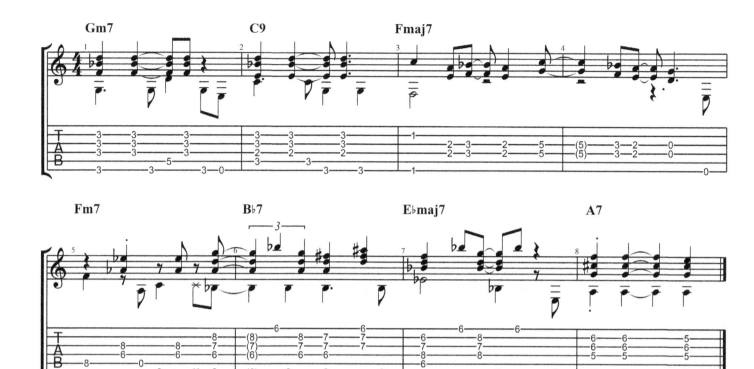

You now have all the components of this tune under your fingers, so it's time to attempt the complete arrangement.

There are a few things to look out for. In bar four I've added a passing Ab7 chord to lead to the Gmaj7 in bar five.

In bar nine, a quick change of chord grip is needed to play the embellishment phrase around the E9 chord. Start with your first finger barred at the 7th fret and play the first string melody notes with your fourth finger. Then switch to barring the 6th fret with the first finger, with your third finger fretting the notes at the 7th fret. (We've jumped from an E9 to an E13 shape).

You may have noticed that I play a more colourful chord voicing for the D major chord in this arrangement. It occurs in bar one, but in bar thirteen as the A section repeats, I showcase this sound a bit more. Here is the voicing I'm using, a more colourful Dmaj7 with a suspended 2nd (the E note on the second string).

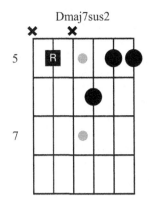

Dmaj7sus2

I like this voicing because it has a very open sound, yet you can still hear it's a D major chord. In bar thirteen I use it to play a phrase, combining it with another colourful voicing in 9th position. It's a different way to play Dmaj9. If you were to hold down the full voicing of this chord it would look like this:

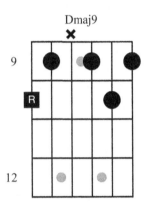

Dmaj9

But because the phrase is played quickly, I miss out the D bass note and play a partial version.

Skipping ahead to bar thirty-three, you'll hear a pedal tone idea that I thought of on the spur of the moment. It's a simple idea: keep a single open string bass note going while the chords over it change. It's a very effective way of creating tension and release in music.

I start with a Dmaj7 voicing barred at the 2nd fret then, while keeping the open D string going, move the barre to the 3rd and eventually 5th fret, playing a melody on the top string at the same time. It's best to understand these chords as Gm/D and Am/D, but if we were to analyse the notes, we'd discover they are both types of suspended D major chords. The important thing is, it sounds cool!

Example 4e

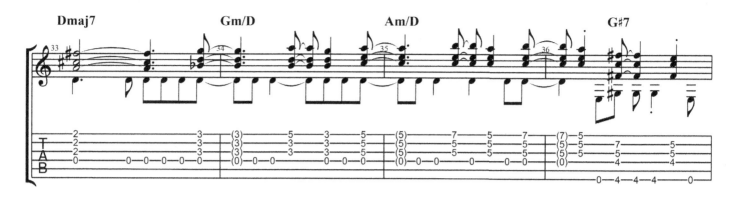

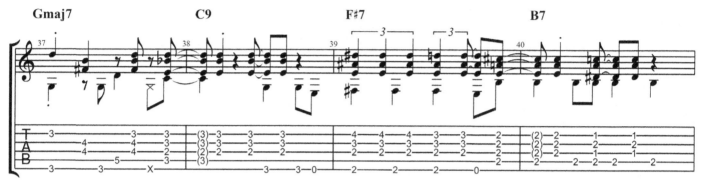

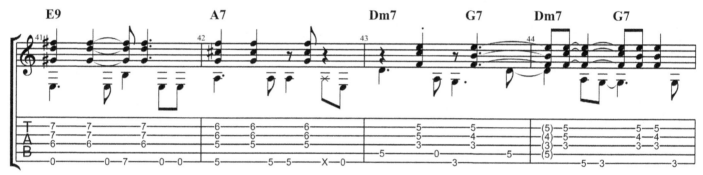

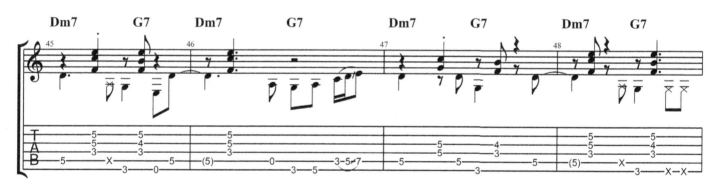

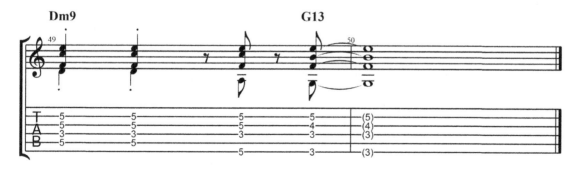

Chapter Five – Corcovado (Quiet Nights)

The title of this composition by Antônio Carlos Jobim, *Corcovado,* actually means "hunchback" in Portuguese and not "quiet nights" as some erroneously believe. It refers to the Corcovado mountain in central Rio de Janeiro, where the statue of Christ the Redeemer stands. English lyrics for the tune were added later by Gene Lees, with the opening line, "Quiet nights of quiet stars" and the name "Quiet Nights" stuck among jazz musicians who covered the tune.

Corcovado has a long form so we're going to focus on one main performance piece. However, I've pulled out a few examples from it to explain my approach to embellishing the comping.

The harmony of *Corcovado* is a fascinating piece of writing by Jobim because it's one of those tunes that completely avoids the tonic (the I chord). I opted to play it in the key of D Major, but you'll notice as you play through the piece that it doesn't actually contain a D major chord! Every time the progression *could* naturally resolve to Dmaj7, it goes instead to Bm6, and so has a dreamy, unresolved mood to it, which is of course part of its appeal.

The first part of the arrangement I want to highlight is bars 9-12. Here I play a chord phrase that forms a short motif. It's similar to the type of call and response phrases found in the blues. The first two bars make a melodic statement and the subsequent two bars echo it.

To play the Gm7 to C7 movement in 3rd position, you can either hold down a G minor barre chord throughout or play the G bass note with your thumb over the neck. I did the latter, but you may find barring easier.

For the F#m7b5 phrase, use the 2nd position voicing you learned for *The Shadow of Your Smile*. Using this grip, the melody notes are easily accessible on the second string. At the end of this bar, when you need to play the melody note on the second string, 4th fret, switch to barring your first finger at the 2nd fret.

Example 5a

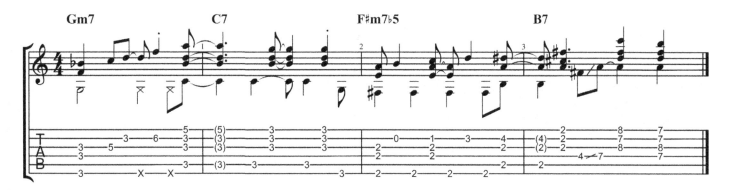

The next time this sequence occurs (in bars 25-28) we want to vary things a little and an easy way to do this is to move to a different zone of the neck. Playing in different areas naturally opens up new ideas, and different voicings will give us access to new potential embellishment notes.

This time I use this chord grip for F#m7b5:

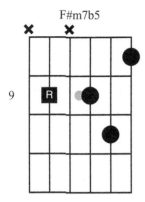

F#m7b5

To play the embellishments, hold this chord shape and move the fourth finger down one fret to play the 9th fret on the second string. Hop your first finger over onto the top string to play the melody note on the 7th fret, then place your fourth finger back into position at the 10th on the second string. Practice this little movement and you'll discover it's quite easy to play. For the B7 chord, I play the 7th fret bass notes with my thumb, but you can barre at the 7th if you prefer.

Example 5b

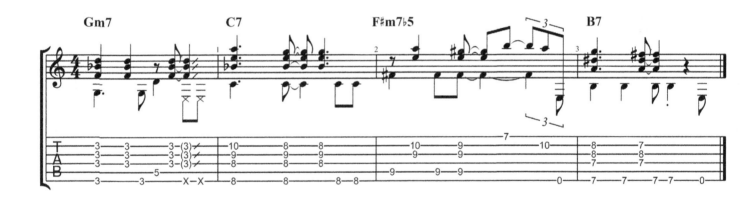

The last part of the arrangement I want to highlight is bars 29-32 and especially the movement from Em7 to A7 in the first two bars, which is a little tricky.

I begin this phrase by holding down this Em9 shape:

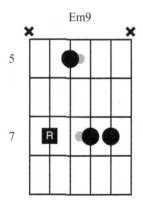

Em9

From here I immediately switch to barring at the 5th fret. This might seem unusual because we're still playing E minor at this point, but we're just planning ahead – getting into position ahead of time for the A7 part of the phrase.

Following the Em9, hold down a 5th fret barre with the first finger to play the notes at the 5th fret on the top two strings. Play the notes on frets 7 and 8 with the third and fourth fingers respectively, and while holding those notes, bring your second finger over the top to play the 7th fret bass note. The brief open low E string gives you a second to adjust your grip to a regular A7 barre chord.

Example 5c

Now we've looked at those details, it's time to try the full arrangement.

Example 5d

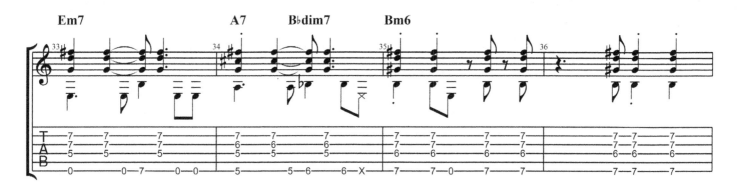

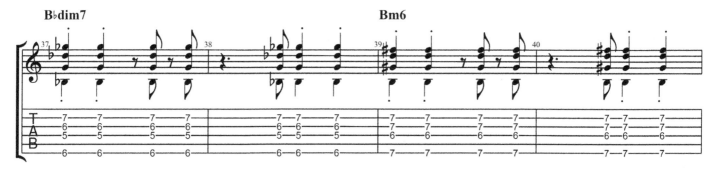

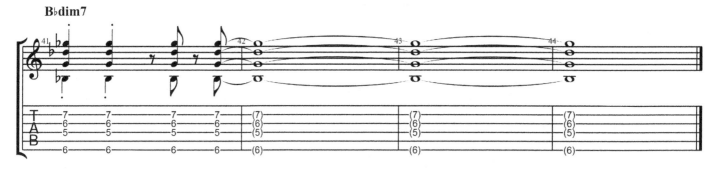

Chapter Six – Night and Day

Night and Day is a hugely popular standard written by Cole Porter and composed for the musical *Gay Divorce* in 1932. Fred Astaire recorded the song with the Leo Reisman orchestra in 1933 and it became a No.1 hit. It wasn't written as a bossa nova, but it lends itself so well to the style that jazz musicians often play it this way.

Cole Porter is known for his unusual harmonic twists and turns and *Night and Day* is no different as the tune begins with a major 7 chord built on the b6 of the key signature! Also, many a budding jazz musician has found it tricky to solo over the descending chord sequence of bars 9-16.

Since it's an essential tune in the jazz repertoire we're going to play a simple arrangement of the whole song.

Night and Day is made up of two long sections: a 16-bar A section that is played twice, with slight variation the second time around. This is followed by a 16-bar B section which includes a repeat of the latter half of the A section in its last eight bars to turn the tune around.

You've encountered all of the basic chord forms already, so it's now case of learning how to embellish them in this new key of Eb Major. I've pulled out a couple of notable examples for you to practice before tackling the full arrangement.

The first example comes from bars 17-20 of the arrangement and is a chord phrase played over the Ebmaj7 bars of the tune that uses a common substitution idea.

It's common in jazz to substitute a I chord with the iii chord from the same key. Here, Ebmaj7 is the I chord and Gm7 is the iii chord in the key of Eb Major. Like most chord substitution ideas in jazz it works on the basis of shared notes.

Ebmaj7 is constructed Eb, G, Bb, D

Gm7 is constructed G, Bb, D, F

The chords have three important notes in common. If you play Gm7 ideas over the underlying Ebmaj7 harmony it sounds like an Ebmaj9 chord (Eb, G, Bb, D, F).

The benefit of an idea like this to us guitar players is that we immediately have a whole other set of chord voicings at our disposal that make the same *sound*. In the original harmony, bars 19-20 are both Ebmaj7, but here I'm freely swapping between Gm7 and Ebmaj7 voicings to create the phrase.

Example 6a

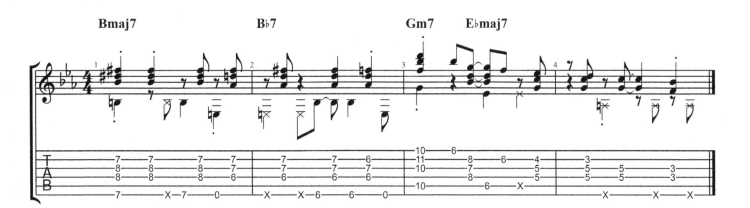

Next, an embellishment example from the descending chord sequence that ends both A and B sections of the tune. This is found in bars 25-32 of the arrangement.

In the first bar, hold down the Am7b5 shape in 5th position and use the first finger to play the melody notes on the second string. In the fourth bar, the Gb13 phrase requires switching between two grips. Here are the two shapes:

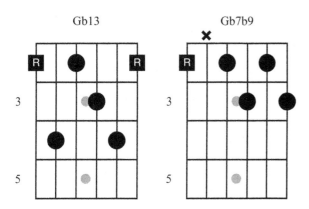

I've opted to play Gb13 as a full barre chord, rather than the stripped-down version jazz guitarists often use. In this instance, it was easier to play a proper barre chord to prepare for what came next.

Hold down the Gb13 shape until you've played the melody note on the top string 4th fret, then switch to Gb7b9 for the last beat of the bar.

Example 6b

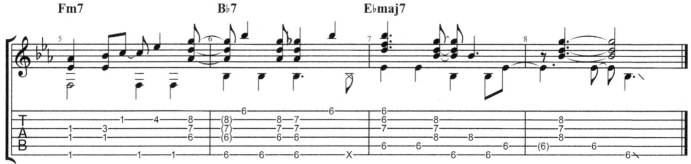

58

Finally, let's isolate the phrase that is played in bars 37-40 of the arrangement. This is an example of how we can break out of the metronomic bossa rhythm briefly to play some single-note melodic phrases.

In the third/fourth bars, I use the idea of interchanging Gm7 and Ebmaj7 voicings again. In the third bar, play the Gm7 shape in 10th position and add the three melody notes that follow it. Then, to play the rest of the phrase in the bar that follows, jump back to 6th position and hold down a standard Ebmaj7 shape. Even though we're just playing single notes, they are all based around this shape. It's useful to keep holding down a chord form where possible, so that we're in position to move onto the next chord.

Example 6c

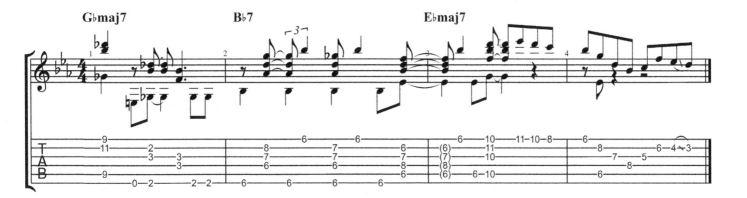

Now work your way through the complete arrangement.

Example 6d

Chapter Seven – Triste

Triste means "sad" in Portuguese. We don't know why, or if, Jobim was sad, but he wrote this tune in late 1966 while staying at the Sunset Marquis Hotel in Los Angeles, as he waited for Frank Sinatra to return from a holiday in Barbados, so they could begin recording their album *Francis Albert Sinatra & Antônio Carlos Jobim* (1967). The song didn't appear on that album, but Jobim and Sinatra recorded it together two years later.

Despite being titled "sad", *Triste* is a bright, uplifting bossa in the key of D Major. It consists of two main parts: a 16-bar A section, followed by an unusually paced 18-bar B section. The B section changes key from D Major to D Minor for its final four bars, so these act as a short vamp to turn the tune around.

Harmonically, *Triste* has a rich chord progression that twists and turns, so it can be a challenge to get your fingers around it. However, there are no new chord shapes to get to grips with – it's just a case of learning to navigate the geography of the tune.

First, let's isolate a couple of the more difficult passages from the arrangement.

The first idea I want to highlight comes from bars 5-8. For the first two bars, hold down a standard 5th position root Dmaj7 shape throughout, even though you're picking single notes in bar two.

To play the melodic line around the F#m7b5 chord, you'll need to make a quick grip change mid-phrase. Hold down a standard 2nd position F#m7b5 shape to begin with and play the open second string and first fret melody notes with the first finger. Switch to the fourth finger to play the 3rd fret note.

Now change your grip and barre the 2nd fret with your first finger. Play the melody note on the second string 4th fret with your fourth finger. You're now set up for the first half of the final bar. Halfway through this bar you'll move to the 7th position voicing of B7b9.

Example 7a

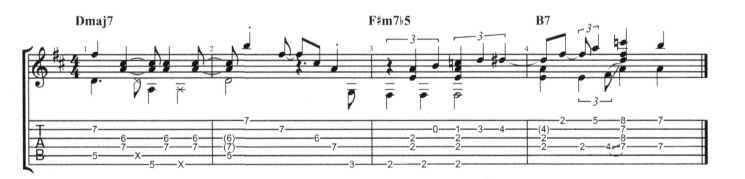

Bars 13-16 of the arrangement are an example of the quick-moving chord changes in this tune. I play the F#maj7 in the first bar with the thumb over the neck to play the bass note. I do the same for the G#m7 in the next bar, but switch to a 5th string root barre chord shape for C#m7.

In the third bar, I switch to playing the F#maj7 in the standard way (first finger playing the bass note), because I know that for the F#m7 phrase that follows, I'll need to barre across the 2nd fret to play the "springboard" phrase that will launch me up to 7th position for the Em7 chord.

Example 7b

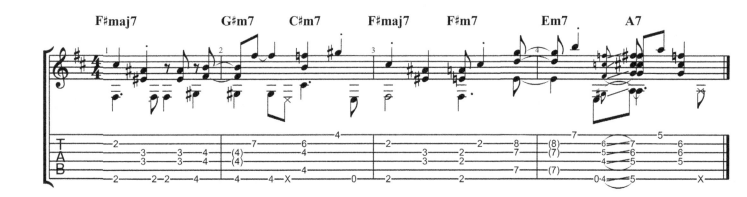

The next example comes from bars 21-25 of the arrangement. The first three bars are all played without moving out of 5th position. Begin by holding down the usual Dmaj7 shape, then change to an Am7 barre chord in the third bar. Still holding this shape, adjust it slightly so that your first finger moves back to the D bass note on the fifth string for the D7. Move to a standard Gmaj7 grip for the last part of the phrase.

Example 7c

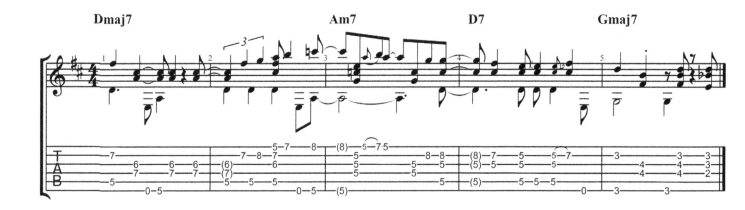

Finally, it's worth highlighting the vamp that occupies the final four bars of the B section. This Dm7 to G7 movement is very common in bossa nova pieces, so it's an ideal passage to practice your skills. Loop this idea around, then experiment to see what embellishments you can add around the chords. Make your melodic lines stand out from the rhythm by plucking them slightly harder.

Example 7d

With those parts under your fingers, now try the full arrangement.

Example 7e

Chapter Eight – How Insensitive

How Insensitive is a Jobim tune that crossed over into popular music and has been recorded by an amazing spectrum of artists including Telly Savalas, Iggy Pop, The Monkees, and William Shatner, along with jazz musicians old and new. Jobim recorded a new version of the song in 1994 with Sting on lead vocals, and Pat Metheny has recorded an excellent version too.

The harmonic and melodic movement of the piece is strikingly similar to Chopin's *Prelude in E Minor*, and some musicians have blended the two together. Laurindo Almeida did just this on an early 1970s live album and prefaced his performance by saying, "If you copy from one it's plagiarism, but if you copy from more than one it's research." Sounds good to me, we're saving the planet by recycling ideas!

By now you know how this works. There are no new chord grips to learn, so it's a matter of carefully working through the chord changes and making the melodic embellishments stand out.

Once you've worked out the geography of the tune, play through it once using just the basic chord shapes, with no embellishments. Then play through it again and add in the movements that will elevate it above a routine run through the changes. I'm sure you'll agree it's a beautiful piece of music.

Example 8a

Chapter Nine – Keep the Home Fires Burning

Almost every jazz standard has been played as a bossa nova at some point in its history. The chord changes of most standards just work so well in this style that it's easy to convert them into the bossa feel. But other tunes that aren't from the standard repertoire also lend themselves to the Latin Jazz treatment and, with some careful reharmonization, can disguise themselves quite well. So, as a bonus, I'm going to teach you my original arrangement of *Keep the Home Fires Burning*.

To give it its full title, *Keep the Home Fires Burning ('Till the Boys Come Home)* was composed by Ivor Novello in 1914 as a patriotic First World War song. Of course, it has nothing to do with bossa nova music, but it shows that any strong melody can be transformed into a bossa nova with careful handling.

I have enriched the harmony of the simple original chords by adding more colour to them and have added a couple of substitute changes. At the beginning, I've added an eight-bar vamp using a typical bossa progression, and this sets the tone for what is to come.

Give the whole arrangement a run through to begin with, noting the chord grips and positions used.

First, just play through the chords without adding any melodic embellishments.

Next, listen carefully to the audio for the arrangement and get the tune in your head. When you're ready, begin to play through the piece, adding in the melody line.

Don't be phased by the fact that there is more melody in this piece. We're applying the same principles we've used throughout this book: hold down each chord grip, then add the melody notes within easy reach around it. If you come across a melody note that's not within easy reach, adjust your grip to account for the movement.

Take this slowly and learn it in smaller chunks before putting the whole thing together.

I hope you enjoy it!

Example 9a

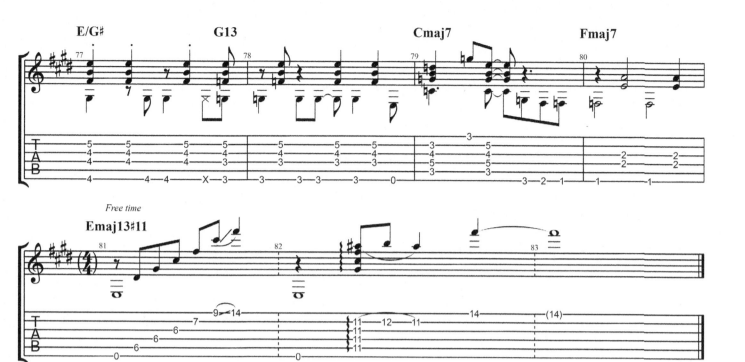

Practice Tips

Here are some final thoughts for practicing your bossa nova comping and converting any tune you like into this style. Once you've produced your own original bossa arrangement from scratch and applied these simple principles, you'll be able to do it again and again.

1. First listen to several recordings of the tune you want to play. Listen to some vocal versions too. The point of this exercise is to get a really clear sense of the melody in mind – plus you might hear a couple of nice twists that the artist has added. The melody is everything, and any improvisation we create should be based around it.

2. Work out the simple chord grips you'll use to play the tune – ideally, simple four-note shapes that will allow a spare finger to add melodic embellishments later.

3. Play through the chord progression and practice keeping the bossa bass note pulse going while you change chords. Lock in the shapes and those metronomic bass notes before you think about adding any embellishments.

4. Once you're comfortable with the progression, begin to enhance the arrangement, first by adding some rhythmic syncopation. Keep the bassline going, but vary the rhythm of the chord upstrokes.

5. Next, add some bass note variation. Create short bassline movements and use passing notes to help you move between chords.

6. Moving on, begin to add some melodic embellishment on the higher strings. This can take two forms: moving inner lines on the middle strings (such as the well-known chromatic descending ideas we've used here), and melodic phrases on the top two strings.

7. Finally, bring it all together by combining all these ideas. To keep from becoming overwhelmed, pull out a couple of bars from the tune and work out a "chord phrase". It might be that you play a high melodic phrase while keeping the bassline simple. Or, you might decide to combine a couple of voicings of the same chord while varying the rhythm. The possibilities are endless. If you can, document the ideas you come up with by recording or videoing them.

Have fun exploring this music, and also seek out some of the classic bossa nova recordings. The more you listen, the more you'll understand the music.

Martin.

Made in the USA
Columbia, SC
21 November 2022

71845092R00046